ZOO BABIES
Sasha the Cheetah

Story by **Georgeanne Irvine**
Photographs by **Ron Garrison**

of the **Zoological Society of San Diego**

School & Library Edition
CHILDRENS PRESS, CHICAGO

Library of Congress Cataloging in Publication Data

Irvine, Georgeanne.
  Sasha the cheetah.

  (Zoo babies)
  Includes index.
  Summary: A young cheetah recalls her early
life and the interesting facts her mother has
told her about her fellow cheetahs.
  1. Cheetahs—Juvenile literature. 2. Animals,
Infancy of—Juvenile literature. 3. Zoo
animals—Juvenile literature. [1. Cheetahs]
I. Garrison, Ron, ill. II. Title. III. Series.
QL737.C23I78 1982   599.74′428   82-9450
ISBN 0-516-09303-7   AACR2

ZOO BABIES

Sasha the Cheetah

When I was a tiny cheetah cub, my mother told my brothers and sisters and me that cheetahs are the fastest land animals in the world! She said cheetahs can run up to 70 miles per hour for short distances. Only a few birds can fly faster than a cheetah can run.

It was very hard for me to believe that I, Sasha the cheetah, would some day be able to run 70 miles per hour! After all, Mother wouldn't even let me walk around by myself. She carried me everywhere by the scruff of my neck.

She often kept all of us babies in a box filled with straw at our Zoo home. Whenever Mother went away, we cubs cuddled together and chirped until she came back. We missed her. Besides that, we were hungry. We weren't old enough to eat meat yet. We drank Mother's milk.

7

Of all my brothers and sisters, I was the most curious. I wanted her to tell us all about cheetahs. What did cheetahs do all day? Were there many cheetahs in the world? Do cheetahs have any animal relatives?

Cheetahs are very special animals, Mother said. Unfortunately, there aren't many cheetahs left in the world because people have hunted us and used our beautiful skins as coats. That makes us an endangered species. Now there are laws protecting cheetahs from hunters.

Cheetahs come from the grassy plains in Africa. Cheetahs who live in Africa spend a lot of time hunting for food. Speed is very important to those cheetahs because it helps them catch their food. They can run faster than any other animal, including the antelope which they often hunt for food.

Lions, tigers, and leopards are all related to cheetahs, but Mother said cheetahs are different in some ways. We're the smallest of the big cats. And our claws are more like the claws of dogs. The claws of the other cats can disappear back into their paws. Our claws stay out all the time. They dig into the ground and help us to run better.

Even after Mother told us all about cheetahs, I still wondered whether I'd be able to run fast when I grew up. Mother told me that as I got bigger and stronger and practiced running, I'd be able to run faster and faster.

The best thing to do, I decided, was to be patient while I grew bigger and stronger. And oh, how I've grown!

Every day my brothers and sisters
and I grow a little bit more. We spend
a large part of our days out in the
grass with Mother. Now she doesn't
have to carry us around anymore.

Sometimes, I leave the other cubs to go off exploring on my own. I always come back in time to eat. At mealtime, my family eats together.

Now we cubs are big enough to eat meat like grown-up cheetahs do. I eat plenty of meat so I will have energy to run fast. I must be eating enough because I run faster every day.

What a proud cheetah I am. Now I know that someday I, too, will be able to call myself the fastest land animal in the world!

Facts About Cheetahs

Where found: In the wild, cheetahs are found mostly in Africa. A few remain in Asia, especially in India.

Family: Cheetahs are members of the cat family, they are the smallest of the big cats. Their heads are smaller than most of the big cats like lions and tigers. Their tails are very long and thick.

Adult cheetahs: When grown, they are about three feet high, with long, slender bodies.

Food: Cheetahs are meat eaters. They hunt and eat various kinds of antelope.

Claws: Cheetahs are the only members of the cat family—including both big cats and small domesticated house cats—that cannot retract (pull in) their claws.

Fur: The color of fur ranges from yellow-tan to light brown. All cheetahs have black spots everywhere on their bodies, except for parts of their faces and under their chins. The spotted skins used to be worn by African chiefs as specal clothing that showed how important they were.

Running: Cheetahs are the fastest land animals. They can reach speeds as high as seventy miles per hour, but only for short distances. They sneak up on the animals they are stalking for food and then take off at a great burst of speed to attack and kill. If the animals have gotten a head start, the cheetahs cannot keep up the high rate of speed and will give up and walk away.

Hunting: Cheetahs are sometimes called hunting leopards. In India they were trained to run after animals and catch and hold them until men could rush up and kill the animals.

INDEX